Put Parents First

Mia Isaac

Activating Our Innate Genius Intelligent Abilities
Parents, Students, Teachers and All Educators: This Is A Call To Action!

Photography by:
Mia Isaac
Daniel Leon Isaac Jamison
Melvin Tobin
Brandon Shell

Innate Genius Intelligence Ability Company
Columbia, South Carolina

Mia Isaac

Put Parents First: Activating our Innate Genius Intelligent Abilities
All Rights Reserved
Copyright © 2009 Mia Isaac
Copyright © all Pictures by Mia Isaac and Daniel Leon Isaac Jamison, son

This book or pictures may not be reproduced, transmitted, or stored in whole or in part by any means including graphic, electronic, or mechanical without the express written consent of the publisher except in the case of brief quotations embodied in critical articles and reviews.

Innate Genius Intelligence Ability Company
IGIA Books USA
Post Office Box 3688, Columbia, South Carolina 29230
E-mail: igiapublis@sc.rr.com

Library of Congress Control Number: 2008943553

ISBN-978-09630229-3-6

Innate Genius Intelligence Ability and the "IGIA" logo are trademarks belonging to

Innate Genius Intelligence Ability, Inc.

First Edition

Isaac, Mia

Designed by Daniel Leon Isaac Jamison, Architectural Drafting, IGIA, Columbia, SC

The author would like to thank Kimberly Epps, computer technology assistance, and the Editorial Staff of IGIA: Doretha Bull, Robin Brooks Belgrave, Patricia Walls and Doshia Scarborough.
I could not do it without them.

Printed in the United States of America

Put Parents First

This book is dedicated to:

Bessie Lou Isaac
Daniel Leon Isaac Jamison
Allston Amad Mitchell
Aaliyah Michelle Glover
Eudora Chandler
All parents, students, educators and other
professional staff of all agencies.

Mia Isaac

Table of Contents

Dress Code 6

Introduction 7
  PART I
  Innate Genius Intelligent Abilities(IGIA) 9
  The Teachers, The Teachees,
    And The Love of Parents 20

PART II
A - Z - IGIA 37

PART III
Projects and Various Trips
African American Monument: Columbia, SC 93
Dr. Benjamin E. Mays: SC 113
Museum of Natural History: NY 117
Ellis Island: NY 117
Catawba Indians Cultural Center, SC 118
Batesburg/Leesville, SC 118
Shady Grove Camp Ground: Bowman, SC 119
Niagara Falls: NY 120
March on Confederate Flag: Columbia, SC 121
Million Woman March: PA 121
Liberty Bell: PA 121
Botanic Garden-Washington, DC 122
White Water Falls: Oconee County, SC 123
Birth Home of Dr. Martin Luther King, Jr. 124
Inauguration of President Barack H. Obama 128
About the Author 131

Dress Code

Parents, let's utilize a dress code for the 2009 - 2010 School Year and beyond.

Dress Code

INTRODUCTION

Parent To Parents - Put Parents First

Who must do this?
Parents, we must put ourselves first as mentors and teachers.

Why? There are over 65 million students of pre-k through college status in the United States. The *Innate Genius Intelligent Abilities* in you and your children are crying out to be activated and used by you individually in your family. You, fathers and mothers who gave birth to children on this earth, were the first mentors in their lives. You must be nurturers and teachers in the lives of your children for thirty years. At the end of each day your child comes home to you. The spirit in the home must be based on love, peace, and healthy discipline. Accurate education must be taught by you parents in each home. Each afternoon you prepare your children to go out the next day into someone else's educational environment and infrastructure. Your child is one of those sixty-five million students.

Read on and learn why these first sentences are stated. Loving, teachable parents are needed right now. This book is written for every human being of every ethnic back-ground throughout this earth. Please do not confront me with whether it is written for one particular ethnic group of Parents. I am a concern parent reaching out to all parents and our children. What is going on in this world right now proves that all Parents are surrounded by the same ills, but these ills are not produced by all Parents and their children. We may have heard the statements "parents are so busy trying to make a living and some parents just do not care" as well as many other labels. Parents, my love, respect and dignity for you and your children will not allow me to list any more. What you must know right now is that children's abilities and skills are not the same. I want to introduce you, your children, teachers, principals, superintendents, librarians, professors and other professional staff, to whom and what they must love and respect. Why?

> *You have watched every level of your child's development.*

"Put Parents First" is knocking at doors world-wide. Improving students' performance starts with you. Improving starts in the home. Your children were born to you. Teach your children to be peaceable. Love your children. You have watched every level of your children's development. Each time any one of us does not teach our children the skills to activate their *Innate Genius Intelligent Abilities (IGIA),* it is like stepping on ants daily and crushing them. No, people are not ants. Yes, our children and the ants have their jobs to do. Children, I need for you to obey your parents right now! That is your job! Children, why should you obey? You are going to become parents in the future. Parents I am asking you to step up to the plate and be excellent parents relative to all of us being imperfect. That is our job! Everything under the sun has been tried except you putting yourself first. It is a family thing. Money can not solve this situation, but it will help. The only people who are making money are those that are capitalizing upon parents who are not putting themselves first in the lives of their children.

Take a lesson from the animals. Parents, please watch the television series *"National Geographic" and "Animal Planet."* The alligator births its babies and carries them in its mouth and later, on top of its back and head to protect them from predators. The snake hatches its eggs and crawls away leaving their babies to fend for themselves. We have learned what both will do when they mature. If you do not know, "National Geographic" and "Animal Planet" will show you what they will do.

IGIA

PART I
The Awakening of The Innate Genius Intelligent Abilities

What do you really want in your life, Parents?
Did you notice that I said "in" not "out" of life?
Why do you want this?
Parents, why did you have children?
Who are you?
Do you know?

What are we like, parents?

How is what we are like going to make our life spiritual relative to some form of education that will activate our *Innate Genius Intelligent Abilities* (IGIA) so that these abilities can be used by you?

Parents, you must give your children thirty (30) years under your protective care for these abilities to be activated and grounded. Your children will be educated by you and others; in the womb from birth, pre-k up and into technical school, college or university, and given C-Grades. Children must abide by the standards that you have set up in your home.

Parents, public school's curriculum changes each time a new superintendent comes into the position. Each one has his or her own program to implement void of recognizing the student's *Innate Genius Intelligent Abilities*. The classroom teachers, parents, and the students are caught in this cross fire. The curriculum that teachers were trying to teach is no longer applicable. The professional staff must learn a whole new string of standards and teach them to all students based upon the grade levels. Teachers' creative abilities are suppressed. Students must fit into the mold and perform. In some districts there are new principals in the school every year, sometimes before the year is complete. Within many of our schools, our students are without certified teachers in subjects such as math, science and others for an entire school year. The students have a substitute teacher. But at the end of each school year standardize tests are given. Parents are told that "your child did not measure up." Who really did not measure up? The children and you are battling with emotional trauma stemming from lack of skills not being taught to your children and you. Thus, the children's *Innate Genius Intelligent Abilities* were not activated for that grade level or subject.

Parents and others remember, all of us must answer to the higher spiritual Supreme Being even if you do not know or want to know this being. Parents, put you first. You are a unique person relative to your imperfections. Your children are unique relative to their imperfections. There is not another person like you or your children. No human being has created in us the abilities that you will learn about from this finding. Your job is to teach your children spiritual and academic education before, doing and after conception. Let's not continue allowing for our children to be without knowledge of the Supreme Being. This Being is love. This Being has power, wisdom and justice. Take a look up in the skies in the night and day. What do you see? Did man create the things that you see? Spiritual education will teach all of us about this Being and why it is a must to get to know, love, respect, and have a healthy fear of the Supreme Authority. Would you say lack of healthy fear has caused much of the ills that we are living among? Why aren't many people that are causing the ills using their *Innate Genius Intelligent Abilities* positively? Parents, accurate spiritual teaching to your child is your job!

Some Parents and some of our Children not having spiritual education to help activate their *Innate Genius Intelligent Abilities* now may cause them to die, go into prison, or other. All of their God given abilities will never be used by them. Our abilities are not for anyone else. They are only for each person. After you have activated your *Innate Genius Intelligent Abilities* and are using them you must help someone else to activate theirs. Parents must put themselves first as teachers to activate their abilities and safe guard these abilities within and for

their children. Thirty -five plus two students and their parents taught me what I am sharing with you. No, I did not know this before I met with these two set of students and their parents or grandparents.

Thank you parents; for trusting me with the educational care of your children. I will always be indebted to you and your children. Thank you mother for continuing to say to me "go and teach in your neighborhood school; the children and their parents need you." Thank you Sovereign God of this universe for revealing to me what *Innate Genius Intelligent Ability* is and what to do. Thank you my educational assistant for praying and teaching me. Thank you principal for saying yes to me; when I presented to you the *Innate Genius Intelligent Ability* curriculum. This innovative curriculum was given to me by the Sovereign God of the Universe for his children. I obeyed the Creator Sovereign Supreme God of the universe and my mother. Children (students) please listen and obey your parents. Parents, children and educators let me share these definitions with you for the purpose of you learning what I mean when I say *Innate Genius Intelligent Ability*. Prayerfully you will understand why I started out talking to you about spiritual education, pre-k through and completing technical, college or university skills. Also, I end my writing on what our children are encountering as they enter the last stages of education. Don't get me wrong, learning never stops.

Innate:
1. Existing in one from birth - inborn.
2. Was and is existing in a person at birth.
3. Concepts present in the mind at birth as oppose to concepts arrived at through experience.
4. Existing in a person from birth, "in born as an essential characteristic."
5. Native to or original with the individual, inborn, natural.
6. To be born in, originate in, existing naturally rather than acquired.

Genius:
1. Guardian spirit, natural ability according to Roman belief, a guarding spirit assigned to a person at birth;
   A guardian spirit of any person supposed to influence one's destiny. Genius is a great natural ability –strong disposition or inclination, great mental capacity and inventive ability, creative.
2. Exceptional intellectual and creative power. One who possesses exceptional and creative power, natural.
3. *Pagan*: attendant spirit allotted to everyone at birth, to govern one's fortunes and determine character.
4. *Christian*: The two mutually opposed spirits by whom every person was supposed to be attended throughout his life. Hence, applied to a person who powerfully influences for good or evil the character, *conduct*, or fortune of another.
5. *Roman*: guardian spirit of a man, a family, or a state. As a guardian spirit of an individual. Notable achievements or high intellectual powers of an individual were attributed to his genius, and ultimately a man of achievements was said to have genius or to be a genius.

Intelligent:
1. Having or showing an alert mind, bright, perceptive, clever, and wise.
2. To see into, perceive, understand, sensible.
3. In psychology, the general mental ability involved in calculating, reasoning, perceiving, relationships,
   and analogies; learning quickly, storing and retrieving information… adjusting to new situations.
4. Having good understanding or high mental capacity, quick.

Abilities:

1. The activated abilities that you will use for work in gainful employment for the rest of your life, giving you faith, hope with wholesome, loving activities in your life and your family.

Innate Genius Intelligent Abilities

The *Innate Genius Intelligent Abilities* are those abilities that are created in you. The concepts are present in the mind and heart at birth. They are born in you. These abilities exist naturally not acquired. With accurate skills taught your perceptive powers, high mental capacity moves within you to help you to learn  quickly, understand, reason, store, apply, and retrieve information. These abilities enable your children to create, calculate, and adjust to new situations. They are your wholesome abilities to be used by you to care for you and navigate your way on this earth. I cannot give you an example of what your *Innate Genius Intelligent Abilities* will be. But I know what they will not be. These are untapped positive abilities that are waiting to be awakened and used by each human being. Do you know how many stars are in the universe? Do you know the name of each star? No human being put these abilities in you. They are not acquired from some other human being. Accurate skills must be taught to you to activate, and develop your abilities void of inaccurate curriculums, intimidation, provoking, academic abuse, emotional abuse, financial abuse, social abuse and psychological abuse by some.

Naming these abilities will only cause all of us problems. Each one's abilities are different. Some people will begin to limit you. Anytime you act outside of your stated abilities, you will be reminded that you have crossed your line of abilities. Yes, these abilities can be altered and suppressed by some that are not honest and some that fear your successful use of your abilities.

Parents, putting you first means that you are obligated to teach your children skills to activate the basic abilities before they enter someone else's teaching environment such as nursery, daycare, pre-kindergarten or elementary school. You are obligated to oversee the educational process from birth up into technical, college or university. Do not be afraid to ask principals, teachers, presidents, and professors of the institutions how they plan to teach your child skills that will release him or her in sixteen or seventeen years into the working world having all of his or her mental faculties in tact. Ask them to explain their grading system to you, even though it is in the catalog. Our children want to work. They need to work. You are the only spokesman (voice) for your children. Have a goal and keep this goal in your mind and heart for your children. Sit your child down and discuss with him or her, your goals. The person in authority (parents, educator and others) whose *Innate Genius Intelligent Ability* has been activated do not feel threatened by another. They will never seek to destroy these abilities in others. They will always work for the good of the child. They love your children and you. They are humble and they are caring people. They will never abuse your children. Again, parents we have the statistic as to what has happen because some parents did not put themselves first, which mean you did not safeguard your children's life and livelihood.

Parents, children need your guidance until they get thirty years old. Parents look your children in their eyes and tell them that you love them; you will provide for them, you will protect them. Teach them how to love, provide for and protect themselves. Do this right now with your children no matter where you and your children are in your lives. It matters! Why? Your children will become the parents of your grandchildren. Our children are ambassadors for us and to the next generation. Better yet, who will our children marry? Parents, you have been entrusted with a human being that has *Innate Genius Intelligent Abilities* born in him or her. There are no exceptions to this finding. The *Innate Genius Intelligent Abilities* are in all of us. All PARENTS that have birthed a child into this system read on because your children will need you for thirty years.

Parents, you need to recognize your *Innate Genius Intelligent Ability*. Have you activated yours? Can you detect your children's *Innate Genius Intelligent Abilities*? Do you know what they are? You should! Do not stop now. **Read** on. Parents, I hear you, "thirty years old, when am I going to have a life?" You will have a better life when you help your children to avoid poverty, drugs, gangs, jumping others, using alcohol, committing sexual immorality, causing sexual abuse, promoting teen pregnancy, acquiring aids, bombing, killings, getting incarcerated, being disobedient, acquiring diseases of all sort, abusing use of authority to and from others. If I missed something plug them in for me.

> If your child is in a gang, it is your obligation to stop the alliance. Children listen to parents and remove yourself out of harm's way.

You are allowing for your children to spend too much time alone and with some whose values are not like yours. Children, you are making these choices on your own or because of your "association." They are not **any** part of your *Innate Genius Intelligent Abilities*. But hopefully it can be corrected. Families, spend time together discussing all of the above. Parental directives must be given by you to your children and children you must apply them right away.

Children, you have never walked down life's road before. I don't know anyone, nor have I ever read of anyone that started the road of life at its end, walked backward into all of life's experiences and ending with a successful journey. You must go through life's toxic experiences and be a success in your life.

Children (elementary, middle, high, technical college or university), you need to listen to your parents, obey and apply all directives when they are teaching  and showing you some of what you are doing and what some people are and will do to you. Pac-Men/Pac-Women are out there. What is best for you? Your parents and grandparents are your first teachers. Spend quality time with your grandparents. Intergenerational interactions are some of the most beautiful sights that your eyes can feast upon. There is nothing like grandparents' cooking and talking. Grandparents and great grandparents have knowledge and wisdom that you will never find in a book, except the Bible. They are excellently skilled and oral history teachers. There are standards in the home that you must abide by if you want your *Innate Genius Intelligent Ability* activated and used. Let us help you children. Good parents and grandparents will not teach or lead you wrong. They love you unconditionally but not certain actions. There is a difference.

Children, you need thirty years to activate and develop your *Innate Genius Intelligent Abilities* and use them. You need to work and enjoy your hard labor. The negatives I listed above were not created in you. Some of you are making choices that are leading to these things. Yes, from conception until you are thirty (30) years old, there is sufficient time to build a successful life without any added responsibilities that were listed above. Abstinence and self control from all the negatives stated in the previous paragraph should be practiced by you everyday. We have the statistics and the verdict is in. It is all of the negatives that we see, hear and feel being broadcast daily. It is a crime for you not to activate your *Innate Genius Intelligent Abilities*, and use them for yourself. It is called "you do the crime, and you will do the time." I am putting before you a new challenge. It is called doing the time now for thirty years (or less if you can pull it of without added responsibilities) or do the crime and time for the rest of your years.

Each person that is alive on January 1st of any year has 365(6) days totaling 8,760 (8,784) hours. What are you doing with your time? It is not too late for any parent to start teaching their children. But, children you must obey. Just do it! Children, if you have already entered an educational institution you well know what I am revealing about C- grades. When you get married you (husband and wife) will inherit each other's debt from the institutions. You start out with money stress. Don't have one baby because you bring that child into this stress. Pray to the Spiritual Being that created the universe and you. Meditate about what is stated here. Finding real wholesome love with someone else in the marriage arrangement is beautiful. This is within your *Innate Genius Intelligent Ability,* also. You deserve to love and to be loved. Money can't buy love. You cannot develop the wholesome love that is created in you because you are being bombarded with so much at one time. Your parents are not the bank and the gas station.

Now, I've gotten that out of my heart and mind. So, let us move on. Regardless of how it happened, the responsibilities of caring for children are the same. So young people, if you have no children do not have any until you have done the time with yourself, thirty years. For the young people that already have children, do not have any more. Do you want your children to enter all of the stress that I have been 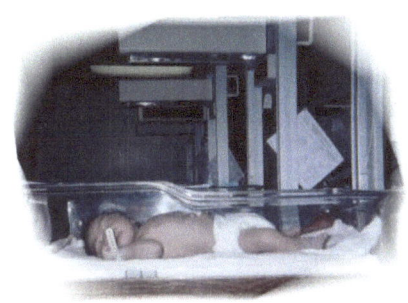 discussing? It is not fair to you, your child or your parents to struggle. There is a world out there that is filled with "roaring lions". They will devour you and your child. Stay focused. If no one has said it to you or if you have refused to listen and obey, let me say this to you loud and clear. **Stay Focused! Do what good parents ask you to do! "You will positively benefit."**

This mechanism is created in every human being by the Sovereign Supreme God who created this universe. All of us were conceived from sexual relationships.

All of us are born with *Innate Genius Intelligent Abilities.* Your babies are born with *Innate Genius Intelligent Abilities.* But it takes love, time, nurturing and guidance for the *Innate Genius Intelligent Abilities* to blossom (develop) and show its beauty. The spider has an inborn mechanism created in it that causes it to make a web. If you inject a chemical solution into it, the spider will still make a web, but not the way it was created to do so. Neither you nor your babies are spiders. I simply used this factual information to prayerfully drive home a point. Be careful with whom you leave your babies. Put your babies in the circle of people that will truly

> **BABIES COME FROM TWO PEOPLE HAVING AN**
>
> *unprotected*
>
> **SEXUAL RELATIONSHIP WITH EACH OTHER** *whether you are married or single .*

love, protect, provide, and care for them when you are absent from them in their crucial years. Too many babies are being sexually abused and killed. You know now that it is for thirty years. I love you. I wish I could teach and care for all of the babies. It is totally impossible. So you and I must pray that other people's *Innate Genius Intelligent Abilities* will be awakened and you will find those persons. They will help you to take care of your babies. Continue to be good mothers and good fathers. Stop this hardship of having babies with five or six different mothers or fathers. You cannot pay child support into these different homes. Your children will not get the full parental teaching and safe guard that should come from both parents. Do not allow for this action to come upon you. In my opinion, this is a form or slavery. This action impedes you from activating using your *Innate Genius Intelligent Abilities*. Young men and young women, hold yourselves accountable until the right partner comes into your life with the purpose marriage.

You are special to me. I just do not want any more young people and babies suffering. I want the best for you and your future. It can happen. Good things can happen, but you must put in the time. Don't give up or give in.

Parents, you must teach your children basic and life skills. How to read? How to write? How to compute numbers? How to use the bathroom and wash their hands properly? How to use the telephone properly? How to help keep the house clean? How to protect themselves from kidnappers? Read to them every day. Show them love every day. These are just a few skills. There are many others that you must teach your children. The basic skills will activate your children's basic abilities. The children will learn, recognize and use these abilities by the age of two. Some will do it before they are two. What I am getting at parents is that you should not send your children into another teaching environment before you teach them the basic skills. They definitely should not enter pre-k or first grade without these basic abilities activated. Your children should enter public school every day excited about the skills that teachers will continue to teach to activate his or her student's *Innate Genius Intelligent Abilities*. You must set the tone for your children to be educated every day Parents. Start by praying and eating breakfast with your children before they enter school. No child should enter school before eating breakfast at home. Try hard to eat dinner as a family. Ask your children every day to teach you what they were taught in school. The word "good" should be replaced with a complete descriptive sentence. Have them write a five sentence paragraph telling you about their Innate Genius Intelligent Ability day. Dress your children in a dress code for success. These are things that you do not have to get permission from anyone to do. Take the lead in bringing together the other parents in your school and agree on a dress code for the purpose of educating your children, saving your children and saving your money. Dress codes will make the public schools act and look as private schools. Quality education activates *Innate Genius Intelligent Abilities.*

The School Improvement Council (SIC) and the Parent, Teacher Association PTA/PTO should be instrumental in helping you. Parenting is your job. Parental dress codes tell the students and the school staff who is running your house. Dress codes tell your children what you expect from them and you are running your house. Your child will enter school every day already prepared to be taught skills that will activate his or her *Innate Genius Intelligent Abilities.* Pull your child's pants up with a belt around the waist. Dress your young ladies in nice dresses, skirts, jumpers and pants. Leave some room in the pants young ladies. It is about activating your *Innate Genius Intelligent Abilities.* You are pretty and you are handsome. Pretty and handsome are, as pretty and handsome do. You are going to grow up and become adult men and women soon. You must learn now how to dress for the successful job that you will get. You cannot force an employer to hire your activated *Innate Genius Intelligent Abilities* if your grooming does not fit their standards.

Parents, make sure that your children have done all of their homework to the best of their abilities. Sign the homework. Children from birth through the end of their technical, or college/university education should get eight hours or more of sleep at night. Turn the television off from Sunday night to Friday night. There should not be any televisions or computers in the bedrooms. Televisions or computers should be in the family room. Perhaps, choose a specific day and time to view video programs as a family unit. Family activities should be planned on days that you choose. Put the child in activities that will develop the child's character, such as walking, running, riding bikes, swimming, tennis, golfing, bowling, basketball, soccer, jumping rope, karate, climbing, skiing, skating, gymnastics, scenic drives, ballet, music, language and any others  that are not stated. Don't take the children and leave them. The person in charge is not your babysitter. Stay with your children from start to finish. Go home and discuss what the children were taught. You and your children must set up physical activities to do everyday. Eating healthy and engaging in physical activities will keep weight under control. Eating healthy will help you and our children to avoid diabetes, high blood pressure, hypertension, cancer, heart attacks and strokes. Mental abilities will be stimulated for the good. Remember, these are our jobs. I am an advocate for you and our children always. Parents, yes I am saying that you must be there for your children from conception through technical or college/university schooling. Thirty years of nurturing and mentoring are a must. Everyone knows that an eighteen year old is not ready for the infrastructures that are out there. They have only been on this earth for eighteen years. What do they know? Bring back the family structure. It is now or never!

All children need good parents who will love them, provide them with safety, security, and accurate directives in spiritual and academic education. These two types of education must be applied in our lives everyday. If you want to be parents, you must have a job, transportation, home, food, clothing and living a clean moral life. We should have already activated our *Innate Genius Intelligent Abilities.* We must use them working and enjoying some of our hard labor. If you have done these things for yourself, don't you think that it would have taken you until you had turned thirty years old to prepare yourself? Children, spending quality time with you during these thirty years are a must. Learning how to manage your money is a must. Can you fit a husband/wife and babies into this before you nurture yourself? Spend some time reading, traveling, meditating about you, the stars, the universe, flowers, water, or whatever you desire that is positive and wholesome. I am always in awe when I look at water. What is it? Oh yes, I am aware of the H_2O formula. But, H_2O does not explain water for me. When my family and I visited Niagara Falls, the meditation about water went deeper.

Parents and educators, when someone asks you if you are employed to help teach and care for their children, accept the job with love, protection, providing for, correct guidance and teaching the skills that will activate each child's *Innate Genius Intelligent Abilities*. Parents and classroom teachers, you must recognize these abilities in your children now from this day forward. So, parents you are and were your children's first teacher, first love, first protector, first provider, first guidance counselor and first skill finder. Classroom teachers, professors and parents must work close together. Parents must reinforce the accurate skills that are being taught by their child's classroom educators.

You were allowed to be the parents of the children that you birthed on this earth by the Sovereign God of this universe. Parents, you must take care of your children in your household. When you send them out into other educational institutions you must monitor your child. Who is teaching them? What is your child being taught or not being taught? There is a call for math and science teachers daily. Teachers and parents in the classroom or facilities such as daycare, pre-kindergarten, public schools, private schools, home schools, technical college or universities are we preparing our children to meet these calls? You were hired to love, protect, provide and teach correct skills and guidance that will activate the *Innate Genius Intelligent Abilities* of each student that comes before you. Teach out of love and from your heart. In my opinion, if you can not from the heart do the above and will not take the high road, then you need to resign from your position after you have read this book.

Parents, some of us have put our children on a run away train. On that train is: abuse, educational abuse, spiritual abuse, sexual abuse, pedophilia, drug abuse, alcohol abuse, verbal abuse, jumping abuse, authority abuse, gang abuse, food abuse, housing abuse, community abuse, and on and on and on. Put you first parents. Slow down! You and your children are the only conductor that can stop your train and get off. Get off now! If you have never activated your *Innate Genius Intelligent Abilities,* you are in a "shaking baby syndrome" environment. Your brain and your heart are asking you to slow down and get off this train. The next train that is coming behind this one is "love, peace, joy, kindness, mildness, self control, goodness, faith, and long suffering." No one can learn for you. Your *Innate Genius Intelligent Abilities* can be activated right now and used by you no matter where you are in your life.

Parents, you set the examples. "When you know better, you do better." For some people the betterment comes too late to do better. When you are in a conference with an educator in reference to your child's education and the conference starts out about the student's conduct, a red flag should go up immediately from you. Discipline and correction for misbehavior must be administered by you parents on the day that it occurred. If you do what was stated in previous paragraphs, I guarantee discipline problems will vanish for the most part. If such happened, it should be addressed on the day that it occurred and not on the *Innate Genius Intelligent Abilities* academic parent and teacher conference. Always asked, what skill has my child not mastered? How can I work with you (the teacher to reinforce) to make it happen?

> **Note to New Teachers**
>
> *Here is a head's up. If you want to be a successful teacher, not burnt out in your first year, get the parents involved from day one. Respect Parents. Pay close attention to the experiences that I am writing about. Parents want to be first in working with you as a reinforcer in their child's education. Parents have goals for their children.*

Teach your children to respect authority. If anyone sets out to disrespect them; the person is disrespecting himself. Whoever is disrespecting the other, the disrespect is in the person who is carrying out such? In my opinion, this is a form of control and abuse. No one can disrespect you unless you allow them to take you into their zone. It is the same as the kidnapper trying to force you out of your area into another place. You will be killed. Disrespect from and by another human being is trying to kill your *Innate Genius Intelligent Abilities*. In fact, they fear you. They move to their authority to control you by any means that they deem is necessary. My father would say, "Give them what they want, but never give yourself." Put space between you and them. Never let your heart dislike them for this. Dislike their actions toward you. Be careful when you are around them and never be alone with them for any reason. Never give your time that you will need to continue to activate your *Innate Genius Intelligent Ability.* Put the disrespect in prayer to the Sovereign God of the Universe who has created both of you and leave it there. The God that created this universe and you sees it and can handle them. Then, tell your parents or someone, everything immediately!

Parents, teachers, and other professional educators, the curriculum that I am presenting to you to teach your children is as easy as the birth pain that you experience, love, ABC, 123, red, black, white, square, triangle, rectangle, phonics, projects and many, many, many other wholesome loving things. Learning is fun and it can make you happy. Parents and classroom teachers, put you first. Learn from this true experience.

The Teachers, The Teachees, and The Love of Parents

The love of parents started with my mother stating to me what the principal across the street from our house would come and say to her almost daily. He asked my mother to encourage me to come and teach in my neighborhood school. "Your daughter should not be starting up her car, burning gas, going off into another neighborhood. There are children right here in her neighborhood that need her talents and the parents know her." My mother believed in me, and agreed with the principal that my "talents" were needed here at home. She drove the play home when she said, "we signed a petition for him because he was already in the building when the other principal retired. He is a good principal and the school is right in front of you." The school was across from my front door.

The truth of the matter I was very, very happy where I was or I thought I was happy. The school that I was working in I enjoyed walking to work almost every day. The walk, I was told, was almost three miles one way. I would meditate deep on things I read, heard or saw. I was happy, slim and trim. I ate healthy. Fruit, vegetables, salads, nuts, tuna, fish, chicken breast, squeezed juices and water are what I would eat or drink daily. Yes, I had to have my one cup of black coffee every day.

I would always pray each day. I must get up and work each day. Working sets the tone for loving and respecting my students and parents. This tone would vibrate into the students. But I saw the need of understanding some of the changes that were being made in the educational system in our district. So, I had a short conference with the principal asking questions about these changes and what I would need to do to be an effective teacher in the classroom. The principal suggested that I learn more about the field of special education.

Put Parents First

I took two courses in the second semester of summer school. It was in these courses where I actually learned the names and requirement for Learning Disability, Emotionally Handicapped, Health Conservation, and Neurologically Impaired. These courses made me knowledgeable and gave me a lot of information about the beginning of the Special Education program. Who would most likely be placed into these classes? Why would the student be placed into these classes? How and who would make the decision for students to be placed? Where would the students come from? What type of diploma would the student receive if they stayed in the program until they graduated from high school?

It turned out that I did not teach in the school right across from my house. I took a position in another school in the district. I had the pleasure of teaching another group of children whom I loved dearly. I often wondered why I always felt fired up when I was teaching children, especially when their abilities would activate from the skills that I taught them. Now I know that it was because of the *Innate Genius Intelligent Ability* within my students and me. My desire was always to see students eyes light up when a new ability would be awakened in them. I always loved to see the smile on the face of the students and the parents when this happened. I knew from the very beginning of my teaching career that I was not putting anything into my students. I just did not have a name for it. The skill that I was teaching was opening up something in them. It was like using the can opener to open a can that did not have a picture of the contents on the outside label. The top comes off and beautiful colorful vegetables are inside! Beautiful, colorful abilities are inside each one of our students. So, awakening those abilities were even greater than this.

It was with this change that I really came face to face with the special education program staff. I had the pleasure of teaching two students whom they thought met the SEP requirement. One student was mainstreamed into my second grade class. The other was a student in my class. The mainstreamer was placed into the program because his mother was an alcoholic and he was awarded to his grandparents. The mainstreamer could read, write and work out mathematical problems on the second grade level. What he missed was maternal and paternal nurturing. So, many times I found myself holding and hugging him. In fact my honest cuddling of the children, teaching them table manners in their health period, and eating lunch with them to demonstrate what they learned led the principal to place him in "your care", the principal's exact words.

Janene (the name of all students has been changed) was the genius who made me respect, fight for and gain as much knowledge as possible within my subject and all programs that came through the board of education to protect my children. Unlike the mainstreamer, Janene could not read, write or work out many math operations. But if it was read to her, she could comprehend almost exactly what had been said or read. Occasionally, she could bring in outside information based upon her experiences. Janene was in the kindergarten group in my class. This group dealt with all of the basic skills, which Janene was lacking, but the combining of the entire class for all of the subjects was where I noticed her "*genius*" ability.

The groupings in my class also prompted me to be very careful about my color scheme. I read an article on how colors enable students to learn. My color scheme was red, orange, yellow, mint green and other bright colors. Actually, I picked up the scheme from my friend and my former educational assistant. It was this color scheme along with the way that I had all of the basic skills information such as the alphabets, phonic blends, penmanship, number line, colors, shapes, sight words, and the students' work that drew attention from others. Their work was always placed on a black sheet of construction paper with a picture framed border around it. Every student's work was placed at eye-level to them. Every student was proud of his or her work. It was this arrangement and students' happy actions toward themselves, their peers and me that drew the special education observers into my class. All of the students' work went up on the "Wall of Fame." Then, we would have lengthy conversations about my teaching style and my color scheme.

A few days later, I was confronted with the case of Janene. I answered the questions with what I knew to be the truth. Janene was a "genius." How did I know this? I began to explain and show all of Janene's work. The special education staff and I talked about all of the teaching skills that I mentioned above. The game was for me to submit an application for Janene to go into the Special Education Program. It was not the learning disability class that they wanted her in (which I was against any type of placement). It was the emotionally handicapped class. I sat through the remainder of the meeting along with her mother without saying another word. As I prayed silently, I made up my mind that I would not be a part of such. You see, I was in constant contact with Janene's mother about her situation. Janene's mother was even to the point of guiding Janene's hand as she would struggle to do her homework. Janene knew that her homework would be placed on the wall of fame for educational excellence. This was the art of education on display for all to observe. She wanted to see her name and her work there with the others. My responsibility was to teach to the genius in each one of my students helping them to rise to the created abilities in them. They were geniuses. Each student is a genius in their own right. I was not going to give my "Pygmalion" over to "Dr. Faust".

My feelings prompted me to request an appointment with the principal. I told him my gut feelings about Janene and the request of the observers. He said that it would not be on my shoulders as to what would happen to Janene. I said to him that "Janene needs a type of teaching that is altogether different from any program that is in this school system." She does not have a special education problem, not according to the terminology that I am learning about in the special education program. He admitted that my being her teacher and with my teaching skills I would know, but he would like for me to talk to her mother and encourage her to sign the papers.

Janene's mother and I talked for over three periods one morning about Janene's placement. She was not very knowledgeable with the program, but she knew enough to know that there was a possibility that if Janene did go into a program as this one, she might never go back to the regular classes. Therefore, she would graduate from school with a certificate, not a diploma. She said "why don't you teach her, Ms. Isaac?" It was in this conversation where I learned how and why Janene was a genius, but lacking all of the basic skills teaching to project such and take the role. Janene's mother began to talk about Janene's birth up to the first grade to me and her great expectations (goals) for her daughter. A greater understanding came to me. The mother explained that Janene never went to kindergarten and by the time she entered first grade, the family had moved five times in one year. I received my answer. A-ha it was true! Janene's problem was not that of special education. The transition of the family had caused Janene to miss out on the most important ingredients of her life. Those ingredients were the basic teaching skills that would have activated her innate genius intelligent abilities. Janene was willing. She had the glow for the love of knowledge. But she lacked the teaching skills to open up that part of the brain that would activate her reading, writing and computing math, to take the role of the "genius". Having these abilities, once activated, would bring her to and on the road to her genius for the rest of her life. The parent was put first as the only voice for Janene.

The mother's revealing some of Janene's background led me to telling her about an alternative program. This program was under the direction of a Jewish Organization. This organization believed and taught that all cases of the lack of learning were not cases for the Special Education Program. In fact, the organizers believe this so strongly that they called this "intensified teaching". All they needed was one month with the child and a cooperating parent. Janene and her mother fitted their criteria. In one month their teaching strategy would tap that part of the brain that would open up for the child and give the child a chance to really work in the area that he or she so desired. The strategy would also prove the organization to be right and much of the Special Education Program to be wrong. The Special Education Program had very few Jewish students in it.

One month, was all that Janene needed. Her mother and I both felt this way. She obtained the information about the organization and Janene's mother packed up her "genius" and off they went for one entire month. I was never told when she would do this. I just began to miss her. During the course of that month I was asked by my supervising principal to replace a fifth grade teacher who was taking a maternity leave. The principal wanted me for this position "because all of the children in that class reading and math scores were very much above level." He had to place someone in that class who would keep those scores high, because if they dropped, the parents would complain. "I know you will do this because of your teaching strategy and I know your teaching background. I will give you a student teacher to help you with the class." All of these students were in the fifth grade. The lowest reading and math level was that of the sixth grade. Some of them actually read above the twelfth grade level. Another teacher took over my little second graders and off I went into another challenge.

As I was walking down the hall one day, I heard someone calling and running toward me. It was my "Pygmalion," Janene. She was back and she could read, write and work math problems. She took me by the hand into the classroom and all of the children jumped out of their seats and ran forward, hugging and kissing me. Tears came to my eyes because I missed them also. Their teacher said "they really miss you." In fact, I could never go around them because they would always stop whatever they were doing and run to me. Janene got permission from her teacher to read to me, write for me and work out some math problems. I could not believe what I saw and heard. All I know is that I was correct about my "genius", whose sparkling eyes and glowing face reflected a happy, bubbling child. She was a winner. She is an *Activated Innate Genius Intelligent Ability* child. There is something about the activation of your *Innate Genius Intelligent Ability,* once it happens, you glow.

Working was not to be a "flow with the tides" for the next teaching assignment. During the month of September, I went into my neighborhood school at the request of my mother and my friend, the principal. The first grade class of thirty-five geniuses, except for about five, came in with the exact educational trait as Janene. We could not believe our eyes or the result that we were getting from the California Achievement Test, Martin Botel Test and Anne Boehm Test. Thirty of our geniuses came straight from home. The five were not far from the thirty. We tried following the curriculum outline for the first grade, but it was stressful. I could not teach to the test. My assistant teacher and I literally sat and observe each student over a period of time. Each one wanted to learn. They were gasping to read, write, compute math, and comprehend what they saw, talk and write about it. The first grade class next to them had their hard back books. Our students saw this and they wanted their books. I was asked repeatedly by them for their books. "Why don't we have our books? When are we getting our books"? They saw outside

and they enjoyed the clean and beautiful areas. They talked about the ugly aspects that they saw also. Something greater was being revealed to me. I had to answer to a higher powerful source. I finally decided to get permission from the principal, my friend, to intensify my teaching. I requested an appointment to discuss my findings.

What was my intensified teaching? I did not know at that time. I knew that I needed to get permission ahead of time. I prayed before I went to him based upon the spiritual conscience behind me. I knew that I really did not have concrete information to present to him my curriculum. I did not have a curriculum to present to him. So, I said to him "I need your permission to do intensified teaching with my students. My desire is to love each student individually and teach them to be successful in their own genius right." I told him the truth. "I can not teach the curriculum that I was hired to teach." The soil would not grow a strong plant. The soil (brains) needed to be cultivated. It needed to be tilled and turned over to wake up the dormant seeds (brain cells *Innate Genius Intelligent Abilities*) so it would produce. He said to me "You are an excellent teacher, go to where the students are." The answer was yes. I said to him, "our teaching will bring them from where they are and above." The spiritual trained conscience was speaking to me. So the higher power, my other teacher and I sat down and laid out our intensified teaching curriculum.

Our students would give us dandelion flowers daily.

My classroom teacher and I could not put anything in them. The abilities were created in them. We had to devise a teaching skill to activate their abilities and motivate them to take charge. **Put Parents First** would be our first teaching skill. Whatever the curriculum would be it must incorporate parents and their children. We would teach: the alphabets, phonics, blends, numbers and their names, colors and their names, shapes and their names, signs and their names, spelling, penmanship, days of the week, months of the year, seasons, sight words, words from every genre, words from their weekly readers, words from their own finding, story time, physical education (yes, put physical education back into schools, dietician and healthy cooked food), hygiene, table manners (we ate lunch with our students), room cleaning, gardening, foreign language (Spanish), musical instruments, music, weekly field trips within the community and throughout the state. We took them out on canoes in Staten Island, to the Twin Towers, the Museum of Natural History, Apple Farms, and other sites in New York. I learned that they really did love to sing. Many of the concepts that we were teaching would turn into a song. We were given this record title, "**Give The Children A Chance**." We worked hard on the skills above. This song became theirs. You will have to hear it yourself in order to appreciate such "intelligence."

It was exciting. It was like the "Pied Piper". Whatever we taught, they learned and they learned it well. By the Winter Break, they were reading, writing and working out math word problems and numbers. Some of them would come to my desk and read notes that the others would place upside down on my desk. The  other teacher and I were ecstatic about such progress. Yes, we began to worry about what would happen to them over the two weeks vacation. We compiled a take - home booklet with all of the work that we had done. We placed notices on each booklet asking the parents to please take time out of each day and teach some of the lessons with their child. We taught the students to teach their parents what they had learned each day. We asked the parents to ask their child to "teach me what you were taught today?" Homework was class work to go. Homework was always the next day's lesson. The aim was that if for any reason the student did not get the homework done at home, they would get it in the class the next day.

How did we put the parents first? We respected and loved our parents. Before we began our intensified teaching we went out and met the parents or guardians of each child. It took us about a week. We went in the late afternoon after school. We let them know what our concerns were, that we need them to reinforce what we were teaching. We asked them to try to feed the children before they come to school, help them with their homework, sign the homework, get them to bed as early as possible, and dress them nice, neat and clean. We discussed a dress code with each parent. We asked our parents to dress our students in white tops and navy blue bottoms twice a week. Dress shoes, sneakers or other were accepted. We asked our parents to dress our students in red or yellow sweat suits for their PE class twice a week (dress codes). Dress codes meant that skill teaching and learning would be taking place every day. The parents recognized right away that they would save money from buying clothes and their children would be learning. Empowering our students and parents to take charge of their abilities and use them would mean happiness. Discipline was not a problem in our classroom. To this day I do not believe in referrals. These slips were not a part of our curriculum. Whether we needed our parents or not they were always available. All homework would be graded and given back to our students the next day to be viewed by the parents and signed. The third day it would come back to us to placed on "*The Wall of Fame.*"

We will need you as we take our children on their weekly field trips. The parents did not need an invitation **ever** to visit with their child in our class. "Come and visit with your child anytime that you want to." Our children always went to another class for a particular subject. We would send notices home by our children a week ahead of time asking our parents to come and have coffee or lunch with us for the purpose of sharing each child's progress with his or her parents. Our parents never let us down. There were always thirty-five parents to represent each student in the class. Sometime parents, grandparents and other relatives would come just to see what the children and parents were so excited about. As I write this now I am still excited.

Our purpose was to have our little "geniuses" return to us with measurable amounts of those *Innate Genius Intelligent Abilities* activated and still tingling in their brains. We had decided before the Winter Break that we would do the intensified reinforcements for two weeks after the students return from the break. After this strategy, we would introduce them to all of their hardback textbooks for the first grade. I can hear you saying "the students did not have any text books?" No, they did not have any books. They could read, write, compute math problems, and comprehend already. They just needed their *Innate Genius Intelligent Abilities* activated. The students did it themselves. We found the teaching skill to activate it. The parents reinforced what was taught in the class room. Everything went just as we had prayed for and purposed. The students were given their colorful hard back books along with a folder with all of their weekly readers in them in order when they returned. I spent the winter vacation placing the weekly readers in each folder. Those colorful hard back books brought about a sound like that of bees buzzing in harmony. To us it was saying, yes, yes, yes, we love knowledge! We have activated our abilities to read, write, compute math and comprehend all of this. We are going to learn about everything that was taught to us. What we read, what we saw, tasted, smelled, heard and felt. It was joyous to just watch them sit at their desk and check out everything. I loved it, I loved it, I loved it! We tested them and we knew that each one of them would pass the test going on to the second grade; in fact, they were above the second grade level. Little did we know that maybe at that very moment there were those planning for exactly twelve of our little *Innate Genius Intelligent Ability* students to be place into the special education program.

In January, a meeting was set up for first and second grade teachers. The meeting was conducted by a supervisor and a special education teacher. The staff sat attentively and listened. The conclusion was that we had many children  who qualified for the (Special Education Program). All we had to do was to refer them. The base team would test and place the students. The teacher made the statement that broke the camel's back as far as I was concerned. "Ms. Isaac, you have Richard, Len, Donald, Jean, Bobby, Sean, Nathan, Joseph, Phillip, Marlo, Joe, and Lindia" (All names have been changed). Everyone was looking at me and I could feel my hair lifting off the top of my head. I heard someone speaking. It must have been many, many seconds before I realized that that voice was mine. I remembered her saying something about being at the "bottom." The word painted a picture in my brain cells, which down to this day, spelled the abyss. We had worked hard to activate our students *Innate Genius Intelligent Abilities*, building their self-esteem, confidence, respect and love in our geniuses. Above all, the students were happy about learning. I remembered saying, "if anyone was at the bottom, it was her and she needs to spend some time learning about all ethnic cultures."

How could any human being use this type of language about another? I walked out of the meeting crying. I went back to my class and went over the names that she listed. There were twelve names. Eleven of them were boys and one girl. I could not contain my spirit, so I went back upstairs to reiterate my statement and cement it. I went on to say "not one of them will I refer, not now, not ever"! We had gained the trust, confidence and love of these children and their parents. Now I would have to go to some of them and lie to them to sign their children into SEP because it seems it would keep the supervisor and many more like her a job. My conscience would not let me. I had already gone through this with Janene. Why couldn't the school system just make sure that the class sizes were smaller; thus giving all children a chance to activate their abilities educationally to graduate from school with a diploma that would enable them to become able, working-class citizens? Smaller class sizes would make more jobs for teachers, educational assistants and total parental involvement.

I had enough students in my class for two other teaching positions. The first grade class next to me had enough students in the class for two other teachers. Altogether, there were four (4) teaching positions that needed to be filled. My mind was moving too fast. I just had to stop it. I had to stop the hurt that I felt. What could I do about my students, the children in my class? I really didn't have any control if the parents were swindled into signing or referring their children.

Too many , I had seen African-American parents and African-American teachers pitted against one another. Usually the African-American parents sided with the system unless they were reared right and could still remember the wholesome teaching that their parents taught them, or if they were like Janene's mother and the main streamer's grandparents. These parents had goals for their children. They loved their children. They knew that something was lacking in getting their children to fulfill the educational goals that they had set for their children. These parents put themselves first by loving, protecting, providing, and keeping their children safe. These parents respected education, trusted teachers who were honest and had a dire need for education.

What would be the outcome? Read the outcome in the book **"I Cry For My Parents!"** As you read the enclosed letter and the response to the letter, you will be able to draw the conclusion for yourself. Keep in mind that this was my "friend" who walked across the street and asked me to come into my "neighborhood school and teach." My friend said, "The parents know you and the children know you. There are children in your neighborhood who need your art of teaching." I learned what the word "friend" meant to  him. It is spelled JOB any kind of way, you can get it and keep it. In a quiet way it was brought to my attention that the principal was over zealous in getting me over there because many of the parents had confronted him about teaching methods, the Special Education Program, positions being held without any children in these classes, and school funds. In fact, they were asking him to leave. I was the ticket for making it possible for him to stay. That was okay. Look what I gained. Thank you, Almighty God, for revealing to me to never take advantage of anyone of my students or their parents. **The Teachers and the Teachees** took the high ground which activated each child's *Innate Genius Intelligent Abilities*. The students left us, entering the second grade with everything that they could grasp at that time. We had our last parent/ teacher embracing before the closing of the school year. We reminded the parents of their responsibility toward their children for the last time. Read, write, math, breakfast, dinner, school dress code, and field trips everyday during their summer break. Plant something in your yard and in your window box. Take them to the library regularly. Tell them and show them that you love them. You will provide for them and you will keep them safe. Do family things - travel around in your neighborhood and outside of your community. Look at the changes of the seasons in the trees, flowers, birds, people and yourself. Always remember that your children can learn, but it starts with you in your home. You must oversee the educational teaching skills that will continue to build on the abilities that have already been awakened (activated).

Parents, classroom teachers, child care workers, technical, college or university professors, it was with these teaching experiences that I was taught by the students and their parents. I was taught the words *Innate, Genius, Intelligent, Ability* and their meanings. The teacher and I did not put anything in any of the students. There is a possibility that we could have altered or suppressed our children's *Innate Genius Intelligent Abilities* forever. The Creator, Almighty, Supreme and Sovereign God of this Universe created the abilities in the students. He revealed this finding to us, and gave us the strategy by which we were to teach the skills that opened that area in the brains that activated the *Innate Genius Intelligent Abilities.* In order for this to work, we had to put each child's parents first and the parents had to feel that they were first in their children's lives. We treated our parents and our students (their children) with respect and dignity. We yield to our students and their parents!

Parents this is your suggested teaching curriculum. Make it fit you and your genius. Your children must feel that you love them, and you will teach them. This is just a guide. Your *Innate Genius Intelligent Abilities* will activate and you and your genius are going to be happy and successful. Parents give them until they become thirty years old. Monitor your children as they are going through technical, college or university institutions. "The scene of the world has/is changing." "You can not put new wine into old skin........" This is another way for families!

Why " C-" Grades?

The activated *Innate Genius Intelligent Abilities* are laying the foundation for each level of their education from birth. Parents, you must prepare your children to move from level to level with these abilities in place. At the technical, college or university level the teaching skill must prepare our children to go into the work world void of mountainous student loans and broken spirits in a respectable time frame. The C- grades must awaken children and their parents to seek other institutions that are not using this grading system before they start. Parents, they are out there and they have your child's best interest at heart. Students never doubt you. Your activated *Innate Genius Intelligent Abilities* may be the answer to one or more problems that we are encountering daily. Pray for "the correct way to walk." Parents, place information in the college records letting the institution know that you are still in charge. I am ending at this level for you and your children's life because this is the end, but the beginning of every thing that will happen to you and your child. Completing becoming a whole, working class citizen starts here.

All you and your children are seeking are to develop their abilities for the purpose of being happy and going to work in four or five years. In dollar amounts based upon what you are made of, how much are you worth? The students start out as a freshman with schedules beginning at 8 a.m., 9a.m., 10a.m., 11a.m., 1p.m. last class maybe at 2 p.m. This is a Monday, Wednesday, and Friday schedule that was set up by their advisor(s). Some freshmen are given up to seven classes on a Monday. One class they will not receive credit. Another class they will receive one credit. Tuesday and Thursday schedules are set up for two to three classes beginning at 8 a.m., 9:30 a.m., 11a.m. and 12:30 p.m. There are other dynamics that play into this. How much time does it take for the student to get from one class to the other? Where are the classes located on the campus? You are late and you can only be late for what ever time is stated? The lateness's will turn into absenteeism. You can only miss a certain number of classes in a semester.

Some freshmen will survive this type of scheduling while others will drop out before the semester is over. Some will finished out their first freshmen semester but never to return to complete the teaching skills that would have activated their abilities. The stress stopped them but their *Innate Genius Intelligent Abilities* are waiting to be activated and used in the field of working. It seems to me that this type of scheduling is a built in burnt out C-, D, and F grading schedule. What is the difference between C-, D, and F? In my opinion, freshmen should never be given a back to back schedule. When your children are given C- grades this will cause your children to spend a longer time than you or they had planned in school. The C- grades cause your children to repeat the same class sometimes more than twice. The repeating of the classes depends upon the infrastructure(s) that is already structured into the different majors in the hands of some administrators and professors within some institutions. Some students are forced to change their major.

This is the hidden agenda that we (parents) and our children walk into. The scholarships, grants, loans and other monies that your child received on their merit while in the public school system to pay for your child's tuition can only be used one time. The C- grades causes the student's grade point average (GPA) to drop. You can only spend money one time. So, scholarships, grants, and some loans (money) are lost forever and the student can never re-apply. If your child's *Innate Genius Intelligent Ability* is still intact within him or her after their first freshman semester, some will apply for a loan so they can continue their education working toward becoming a working class citizen. Why do parents and their student apply for a loan? The grants and scholarships are not given to them because of the C-, D and F grades that was given to the students in their freshmen, sophomore, junior and senior semesters. The loans put the students in a cycle for the duration of their technical, college or university stay. In my opinion the game plan is or was for the students to get a loan, the institution to get paid first and do not pay any matching scholarships to students. Some parents and their student obtain these loans because they have goals. So, by the time the student completes his skillful education he or she comes out with a degree and accumulated loans (debt) and interest in the amount of $100,000 or more. This can happened in three to five years. Your child graduates from high school debt free yet in four to five years he or she is in debt for the above amount or more; thus, becoming a victim of the $16 billion, or more student loan debt. This is **Academic Economic Slavery (Slave-onomics)** in my opinion.

Will he or she get a job to balance out their loans? Will he or she be able to pay on school loans, rent or mortgage, car payment and some food? You can only spend money one time. So, parents maybe now you will understand why you need to give your children until they get thirty (30) years old to fully activate their *Innate Genius Intelligent Abilities* to become a whole, working class citizen. Children, maybe when you and your parents discuss all of this early on you will understand why you must obey your parents and others that have your best interest at heart. You must work. When you work in the field that you like, you will enjoy your work, be happy and a responsible worker.

Parents our children need to be nurtured by you through the many blows that he or she will encounter throughout these thirty years. Actually it seems to me that the C- grades are a form of academic economic slavery, emotional abuse, and planting doubt in the mind and heart of the student. It seems to be a ploy by the educational institution to receive money. The loans give them their money first, and it is a continuous thing to get money from parents and the students. The loan institutions receive their payment with interest. Some students are repaying college loans and student loans with interest. Don't get me wrong, I am not saying that all degreed persons are using their *Innate Genius Intelligent Abilities*. Some of them have never activated their *Innate Genius Intelligent Abilities* because they do not know what it is. Some of them can easily give C-, D, and F grades because of their own fears. The master always made the slave fear that he was dumb. According to the master, the slave did not know anything. But the slave could draw up the blue-print and build the lay-out according to the blue-print of what he was told to construct. What is the difference between the master and some administrators and professors? What is the difference between C-, D, and F grades? If these grades are given to our children at the end of the semester, our children will have to repeat the class or classes. The institution, administrators and professors get paid two or three times for the same classes. The same professor is teaching the class again.

Students do not have an opportunity to choose another professor because there is only one teaching that subject. "Transfer the student to another institution?" That is not an option. There is something wrong with this picture. Our children get nothing but debt to pay back. The masters receive payments monthly and yearly even if the students drop out or graduate.

If your child finishes (or not) he or she will be in debt to student loans for the rest of their lives because he or she has stayed in school two or three years longer than the semesters outlined by the grade advisors doing orientation. The freshman schedule was set up by the advisors. If the student does not complete the teaching skill, he will be in debt for the rest of his life, thus a stressful life start - **Academic Economic Slavery.** This is the academic economic slavery's share-cropping system. "People use to pick cotton. Now our students and parents are the cotton." Out-of-state tuition should be abolished immediately. The child was born in America. Forgiveness should be given to all student loans. Our students are in too much debt. We send our children to technical, college or the university to be taught and trained to go to work in four to five years. Stress is keeping our children from fully activating their best *Innate Genius Intelligent Abilities.* Some children are returning to their parents limping. Sometimes, they are crushed forever. What happens to the *Innate Genius Intelligent Ability?* Can it be rekindle? How? If our children really cannot measure up, then we need to take a good look at all parents in all fifty states and throughout the world. Parents must look at what we are teaching or not teaching our children spiritually and academically in the home. Everyone must look at what the public schools curriculum are teaching or not teaching immediately in all fifty states. Parents must look at what the technical, college or university infrastructure is really about. You are dealing with brain cells that are greater than you or the curriculum that you are trying to teach.

Solutions: Activate your Innate Genius Intelligent Abilities from 2009-onward

Parents, "If we blunder raising this group of children nothing else will matter." These groups of children have *Innate Genius Intelligent Abilities* that are untapped. Parents, get involve and stay involve with your children. Children, obey your parents. I obeyed my mother and I taught in my neighborhood school. The paycheck that I received was of serving children and their parents with skills to help them some day to become a whole, working-class citizen. In my teaching, the *Innate Genius Intelligent Ability* was revealed to me. Yes, we must get paid so that we can pay for our food, shelter, clothing, and provide for the family that we will take on. Your parents must not take care of you forever. Any children that you become a parent to, must be loved and cared for by you. All of us must prepare ourselves first. Have you ever taken the time to watch the sun going down? It is such a beautiful sight until I feel as though I can smell it. The sun's aromas for me are untapped. Be a family!

Children you are not thugs. Rise to the level of your *Innate Genius Intelligent Abilities*. How much are you worth in dollars or money? Am I saying you do not need money? No, I am saying that as of this second, let's stop allowing people, agencies and institutions to make money off of us. We are dollars to some of them.

What have I learned throughout the years? Millions of dollars can never measure up to our God Given Abilities. But we must get a pay check. Classroom teachers and professors, some of you, must do the right teaching. There is no dollar amount that could pay for the feelings that I have now and when I taught my students the skills that activated their abilities, which at that time was for them to read, write and compute mathematical numbers. A solid foundation was laid for all the abilities that were in our students to be activated from grade level to grade level and used by them only. The parents of each child had to remember to put themselves first in safeguarding these abilities. Parents must get involved and stay involved for thirty years. You must be a mentor for your child and ask for a team mentor. Children (students), you and your parents are your first role models.

Our son is twenty-one years young now. I have had the opportunity to teach him about his *Innate Genius Intelligent Abilities* and spiritual education. The teaching has come full circle for me. So in August 2006 when the phone rang, and our son's voice was on the other end; our son's voice told me something was not right. I listened and prayed while he was talking to me standing in the office of the professor or advisor. Immediately, the voice behind me, my spiritual conscience revealed that his *Innate Genius Intelligent Abilities* were being attacked, and it also revealed why? I said to him "thank you for obeying the teaching that you received in the womb and throughout your life on this earth. It is not your job to handle this." I saw our son's character in play that day. "This is your third week into all of your classes. Put the professor or advisor on the phone and you return to your class."

All parents, teachers, professors and others must work together. Our children deserve the best possible education and the best possible parents. Education starts with parents. Your fulfillment, your worth and you, are in your *Innate Genius Intelligent Abilities*. Parents, we must put ourselves first in teaching our children moral, spiritual, physical and mental education. Start in the womb, and it is never too late to start wherever you and your children are in life. Let me celebrate and honor all parents and their children, now! No parent must be left behind! Basic skills taught accurately opens up basic *Innate Genius*

Intelligent Abilities from grade level to grade level. Activated basic abilities are ready to receive the information highway all the time and apply these building blocks of abilities from grade level to grade level. READ! Parents, "Ask not what others can do for your children. Ask, what can I do for my child." Parenting starts with us parents and it ends with us. We must respect and dignify other families. Activating your *Innate Genius Intelligent Abilities* and using them are about you and your family. But it is also about you and other families. Our children want to work and get paid the accurate amount of money for their work. "You can not put new wine into old skin." Let's come together for the purpose of activating our children's *Innate Genius Intelligent Abilities* parents and teachers. People are not the same but they are the same in the activation of their IGIA in respect to life, liberty and pursuit of happiness. Parents, you must believe in yourselves and your children and help your children to believe themselves. It all comes together to make one big happy, READING family.

1. Parents, read to and with your children every day.
2. Parents, put your children in a dress code (pre-k through the end of technical, college or university education).
3. Parents, feed your children breakfast and pray with them everyday before they enter school.
4. Parents, help your children with their homework and sign it.
5. Parents, reinforce what your children are taught in school and in the home.
6. Parents and teachers, attend all Innate Genius Intelligent Abilities workshops.
7. Parents, develop/practice a positive value system with yourselves and your children.

Kenneth and Daniel have been friends from elementary school. They are still friends and are still without added responsibilities, 2005 Graduates.

Aa

Aa *is for ancestors.*
Teach me about my ancestors,
algebra, architect and the antarctic
so I can have a stronger
beginning in my life.

Allston

Aaliyah

How many chairs do you see?

What color are the chairs?

Aaliyah & Allston Learn the Alphabets, Numbers, Colors, Shapes, and their Names.

Bb

Bb *is for Buba.
An African Dress.
B is for Biology,
bank,
bacteria, and
business.*

Put Parents First

African American Baskets from South Carolina Low Country.

Dr. Charles V. Bolden, American Astronaut from Columbia, SC encourages Daniel to complete his goals.

B is for band: Eau Claire High School Band

"No Half Stepping"
Director:
Mr. Myron Thomas

Cc

Cc *is for chemistry.
Teach me chemistry, cornrows,
calculus and care.
I need these skills taught
now so my innate abilities
about these words in the future
will be activated and made easier
in my educational growth.*

Do you know where milk comes from?

Cows

Dr. Benjamin Carson, World Health Surgeon autographs his book for students.

In the early 17th and 18th Centuries, cotton was King in the Southern States.

Dd

Dd *is for dress code. I will learn better when and if my mind is not on the latest style. My attention must be on the subjects that I am being taught. Dad and Mom you are responsible for setting this example and sending me to school dressed for success.*

Put Parents First

D is for Daniel,
a young student
bound for success.

D is for Dinosaur at the
Museum of Natural History in New York.

D is for Drum.

Ee

***Ee** is for education. Educating me, Dad and Mom is the first step in my life. You must teach me and expose me to the world around me. You must teach me how to eat healthy, how to embrace the environment, ecology, to drink plenty of water, exercise daily, walking, and sleeping for eight hours each night. Ethamology what is that?*

Daunya' Stands under the Elephant Ear plant.

Environment and how children learn about turtles.

Adults teach youth how to respect the Environment.
How to fish for crabs.

Ff

Ff *is for food. Feed me plenty of proteins, fruits, nuts, vegetables, milk, some juices and water. The nutrients from these foods will enable me in my health and to learn about my family, French, Fahrenheit, and names of flowers.*

Family Reunions are Important for teaching oral history.

Tom Feelings World Artist autographs his work for students.

Fruits of Labor

Gg

Gg is for graduation. Dad and Mom help me to graduate with a diploma, and a degree. I must have a proper degree to enter the next step in my life's work. Geography, graphs, geology, and goals are subjects I will need for technical, college/university and the world.

Graduation Day

The beginning of my preparing to become a whole, working-class citizen.

G is for graduation – Eliscia

G is for graduation – Jordan

G is for graduation – Terrell

G is for Graduation - Robin

Hh

Hh is for hands. My hands are my created, built in tools. Teach me how to use them for success in my life. From conception, my health, hands, heart and head are very important for you and I to safe guard.

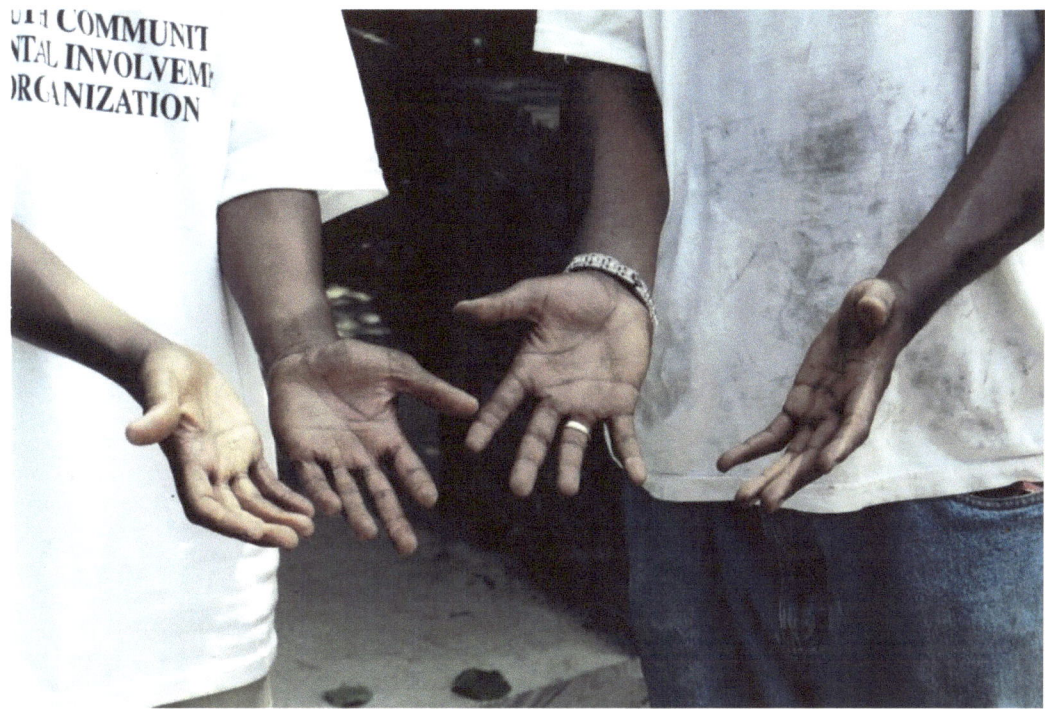
Helping hands need guidance.

Families lived in these tin houses until 1998 in Batesburg, South Carolina.

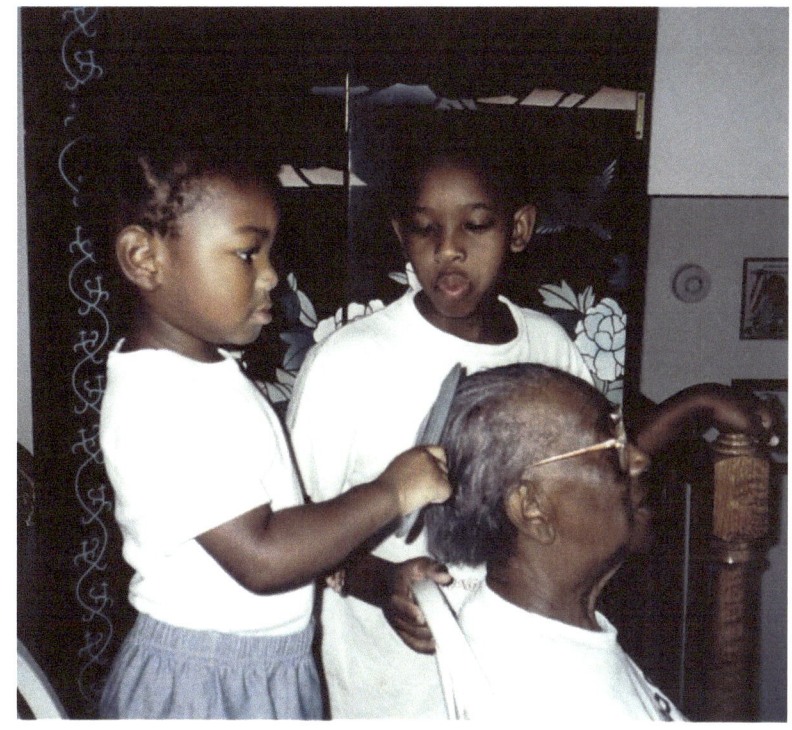
Combing Great-Grandmother's hair bonds children, one generation to the next.

Ii

Ii is for Innate. I am born with Innate Genius Intelligent Abilities. Do not tamper with it. Do not allow for others to tamper with it.

My life and my livelihood depend upon it being activated and used by me only.

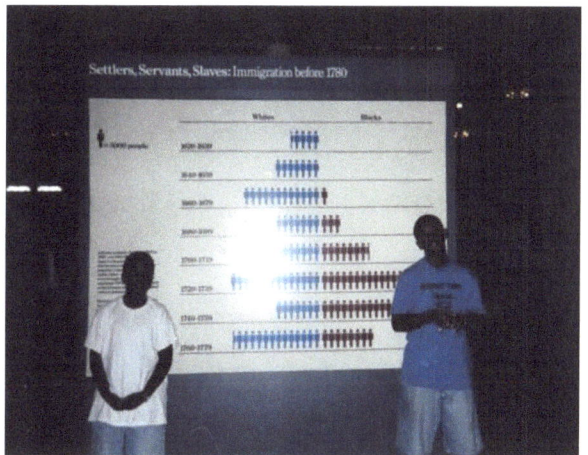

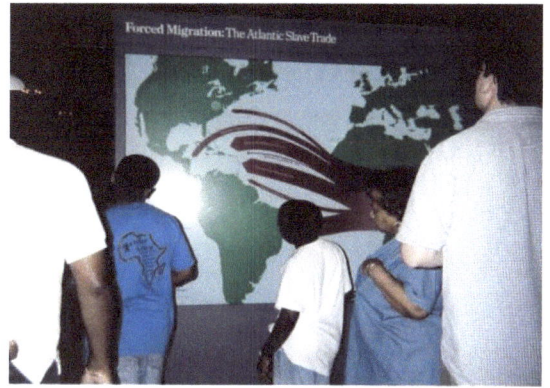

Ellis Island in New York is where most European Immigrants came into the United States of America.

Catawba Indian House

Jj

Jj is for Judge. Do not judge me.
But if you must, judge me by the content
of my character and not by
the color of my skin.

Young people from all over the United States meeting each other and learning as they attend the National Young Leaders Conference in Washington, DC.

Judge and Mrs. Finney of South Carolina at the unveiling of the African-American Monument.

Kk

Kk is for King. Dr. Martin Luther King Jr. is one of the leaders of the Civil Rights movement. One man or woman does make a difference.

Birth place of Dr. Martin Luther King, Jr. in Atlanta, Georgia.

The Memorial and Eternal Flame - a tribute to Dr. Martin Luther King, Jr.

Ll

Ll *is for love learning. You teach and I will learn everything that I will need in my life. No one can learn for me, but I do need your skills that will teach me laughter, language, and light. These are essential ingredients for learning.*

Statue of Liberty

Learning

Mm

Mm *is for Music. Soul, classical, symphony, rhythm, and rapping are music. Violin, piano, bass, guitar, saxophone and keyboard are musical instruments. You must expose me and allow for me to learn how to play the different instruments.*

DuSable Museum in Chicago, Illinois. DuSable was the founder of the City of Chicago.

Student practicing the Bass Musical Instrument

March against the Confederate Flag in Columbia, South Carolina – January 17, 2001

Nn

***Nn** is for no. Teach me to say no to drugs, alcohol, sexual immorality, gangs, and anything that will stop me from becoming a healthy, successful, spiritual-minded, working-class citizen. I have skillful abilities.*

Parents, expose your children to positive things.

Parents, spend positive, wholesome time with your children.

The bird's nest.....How many bird eggs are in the nest?

Family visiting Niagara Falls on the New York side.

Oo

Oo *is for opportunity. Do not say that I have failed when you have blocked all of the opportunities for my survival. Entrepreneurship, ownership, and Leadership are for me to set goals to achieve.*

"These children were taught the IGIA Skills"

Innate Genius Intelligent Ability
teaching changed the lives of the
children and teacher in this picture.

Grandma, What is Powder?

Pp

Pp *is for healthy pride. My being alive gives me great pride and dignity in being a member of my family. Pride is why my head is up and my eyes are in contact with yours. Philosophy, physics, psychology, and physical education are subjects I must learn.*

Penn School in Beaufort, SC

The First Black School in South Carolina

Captain Estell Young and grandson, Justin

Policeman: Teach your children to respect authority.

Qq

Qq is for questions. Our children must be encouraged to ask questions. Answering questions help our children to developed their Innate Genius Intelligent Abilities.

Qq is for quest, quilt, quotient.

Put Parents First

Quilts are exhibited at the Martin Luther King Center in, Atlanta, Georgia.

The Youth and Parental Involvement Organization

Rr

Rr is for reading. Teach me how to read. The innate ability is created in me. Parents, you must find the skill that will activate my reading ability before nursery or you place me in any other educational setting. I am curious about everything. I must learn how to read before I embark upon someone else's teaching. Remember, you are my first teacher to activate my Innate Genius Intelligent Abilities.

Reading starts from the cradle and is used all through life.

Reading expands our mind, gives us faith and fosters our hopes.

Raven Simoné says,
"I Love to read!"

Ss

Ss is for success. Some of us had ancestors that were very successful in the past. Written laws prohibited them from copyrighting, patenting, and claiming these successes. Science, Spanish and Social Studies are subjects I need to learn. Teach me about them.

Shady Grove Campgrounds in Bowman, South Carolina

"Slave Retreat after the Harvest"

There were 119 houses built in a circle.

A slave retreat built as a place where slaves could renew themselves spiritually and physically after the harvest.

Tt

Tt is for teaching. Teach me about all cultures so I can sit down at the table of cultures with others. I am eager to learn.

Trigonometry, task, theatre, and tuba are all words beginning with the letter T.

Twin Towers at the World Trade Center in the background

The Statue of Liberty

T is for Teacher

Uu

Uu is for understanding. You cannot teach me if you do not love me, understand me and know something about my innate ability.

Ukulele, Urine, Utility, and United are "U" words.

Can you name some other words beginning with the letter "U"?

Put Parents First

Hi, I am having fun in a "U" shaped tree limb in Beaufort, South Carolina.

Vv

Vv is for values. I must be taught proper values from conception. These values will travel with me into my life, my home and my family.

Other words beginning with the letter "V" are virtue, vitality, volume, and vertical.

Beautiful View

"Did you plant vegetables in your garden or flowers?

Ww

Ww is for will. Where there is a will there is a way.

Witness, wonderful, weaver, weigh;

Now, you think of more words beginning with the letter "W".

 Roger Wiley was principal of Arden Elementary School in Columbia, South Carolina. Some Principals can and do make a difference.

White Water Falls and Devil's Fork
Oconee County, SC

W is for Winter.

Xx is for signature. Did you know that many in the past history could not activate their innate abilities to write. Some of them made an X instead. These are some X words I must learn. X-ray, xylophone, and Xerox are X words. How many "X" words can you find?

"Grandma,
will you teach me how
to write my name, so I
won't have to make an X ?"

Yy

Yy *is for young. I am young. I am gifted. I have abilities. Find the educational skill(s) and tool(s) that you need to teach me how to activate my Innate Genius Intelligent Abilities.*

Y is for youth. - Daniel Jamison

Zz

Zz *is for zeal. Parents, put yourself first in the lives of your children. You demonstrate zeal for and to them. Zealously teach them the positive things that you know. Look them in the eyes and tell them "I love you." "I will protect you." "I will provide for you." "I will keep you safe."*

What are other "Z" words?

Zz is for zeal: Grandma, you have such zeal for life.

Jermaine O'Neil is a graduate of Eau Claire High School and an NBA basketball player.

Grandma Bessie's Garden

Mia's Flower Garden on the porch

My flower (Zinnia) Chair
If this chair could talk!

PROJECTS

Parents, you are responsible for exposing your children to people, places and things in the world around them. Read with them every day. Travel with them through the pages of a book as well as scenic drives. Take them on scenic trips to see, feel, touch, taste, and hear what you have read together.

Start your projects in your own house. Clean it up. Teach your children to clean their room, bathrooms, kitchen and other areas. Just a tip, remove the clutter from your room and the children's room. Turn your dinning room into your dinning room library especially if you still have children in school. Provide book shelves for their books. Make their library inviting to them. Treat them to at least a book a month or more if you can afford it. Read the books together.

Take them to the public library often. Beautify your yards back and front if you have one. Beautify your window sills with flowers if you can. Plant a garden together. Where ever you live beautify it. Pick up the papers on your floors and in your yards. If you are using profanity, clean out your heart and your mouth will speak *Wholesome* language.

Youths, your pants are not down or too tight because we asked your parents to put you in a dress code. Technical, college/university students, you are dressing for success everyday because you are on your way out into the work force, either as a entrepreneur or hiring your activated *Innate Genius Intelligent Abilities* out. Use your *Innate Genius Intelligent Abilities* and construct a project with your family. These are suggestions. Your *Innate Genius Intelligent Abilities* should not lead you to do the exact things that I have suggested. You will do much more and better.

The African-American Monument was designed by
Mr. Ed Dwight, sculptor of Denver, Colorado.

The African-American Monument site is located on the East Side of
the South Carolina State House grounds.

The African-American Monument

The African-American Monument was a project that we took on from 1999 until it was completed. Please see the photos through our eyes. The photos are set up in chronological order, the way I saw it as I visited. Would you like to know what was in the circle before the monument? How was the monument built? Why is it important for you to meet the architect that constructed the blue-print for the monument? Who is he? Where is he from? Where can you find the monument?

View the pictures and visit the location if you have not already. The African-American Monument is located in Columbia, South Carolina on the grounds of the State Capitol. It was unveiled on March 29, 2001.

These are scenes that you will never see happen again. As a free-lance photographer, I took the pictures to share with you and your family. I hope that you will enjoy them. Parents, take your children to the monument and encourage them to write about their experience and what it means to them.

The architectural blue-print and the replica of the monument were constructed by Mr. Ed Dwight, Sculptor of Denver, Colorado.

IGIA

The African-American Monument was designed by Mr. Ed Dwight, Sculptor. He captured the essence of the effects of slavery from 1619 - onward.

A view looking East from the East entrance of the South Carolina State House before the ground-breaking

This is the day of the "Ground Breaking" for the African-American Monument.

Photograph contributed by Daniel Jamison

Mrs. Bessie Isaac, Mr. Ed Dwight, Sculptor and Mia

Mr. Ed Dwight, Architect with his replica of the African-American Monument

Author communicating with Representative Gilda Cobb-Hunter at the African-American Monument's ground-breaking

Youth and grandparent getting autograph of Judge Finney as they all view the African-American Monument replica

Daniel and Grandma view the African-American Monument with State Representative Gilda Cobb-Hunter.

Put Parents First

Put Parents First

Put Parents First

The Marker for the birth place of Dr. Benjamin E. Mays.

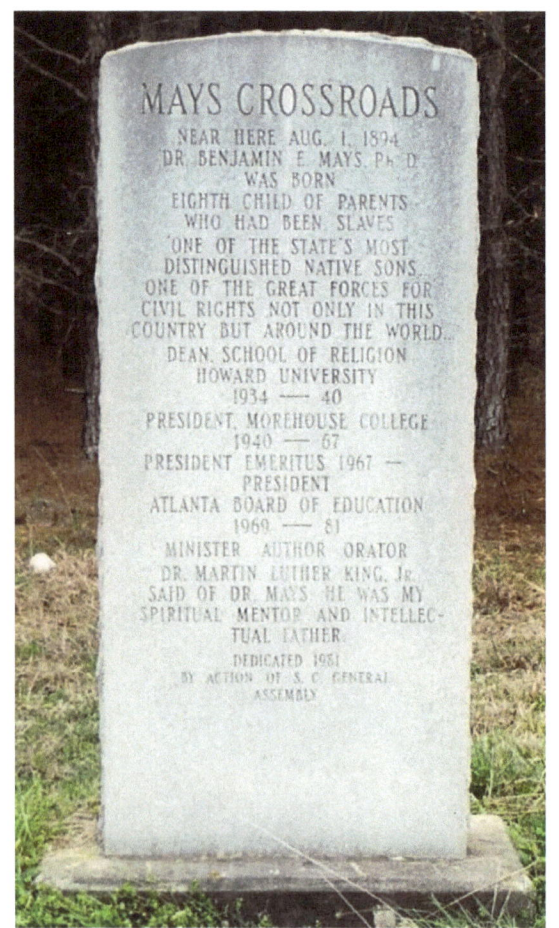

Dr. Benjamin E. Mays

Read the historical marker that I have photographed. I have pictures of the Dr. Benjamin E. Mays birth place, the cabin. You will never get to see this again and neither will I. The cabin is not there any more. But we saw it with our own eyes. The pictures are proof of the location. Parents, you and your children should do research on Dr. Benjamin E. Mays and learn more about him. Read, write and discuss your findings as a family.

Dr. Benjamin E. Mays' parents were slaves in the state of South Carolina. Dr. Mays was born in the house that you see. He struggled to gain the skills that activated his *Innate Genius Intelligent Abilities*. He became President of Morehouse College in Atlanta, Georgia from 1940-1967 and on the Board of Trustees at Benedict College, Columbia, South Carolina.

Take on a project as a family where ever you are. Invite other families to come with you. Prepare a good delicious dinner before you take your scenic trip. Bake some potatoes pies for desert. It is fun especially at the end of the day when you are sitting at the dinner table eating and discussing your findings. Set it up ahead of time.

ABC are for my parents and me. I love you my little IGIA's. Activate and develop your Innate Genius Intelligent Abilities and use them to take care of you from 2009 onward. Teach someone else about theirs. Learn to love all people from your heart.

Project:
Dr. Benjamin E. Mays

Grandma Eloise and granddaughters

Jordan and Daunyá are standing in front of gate before Dr. Benjamin E. Mays' birth place.

Two students of the Youth & Parental Involvement Organization witnessing the site.

Morehouse College in Atlanta, Georgia

A visit to the Museum of Natural History in New York

A visit to Ellis Island

Catawba Indian Cultural Center

Catawba Indian Cultural Center Director, Wenonah G. Haire; Rock Hill, S.C.

Tin Houses that families lived in up until 1998 – Batesburg/Leesville, South Carolina

Shady Grove Camp Grounds, Bowman, South Carolina
The horn is being blown by the oldest living
member at the time, Mr. Johnson.

Penn School, Beaufort, South Carolina

The waterfall to the left is Niagara Falls, United States, and in the far background is Niagara Falls, Canada.

January 17, 2001
March against the Confederate Flag - Columbia, South Carolina

Million Woman March
Liberty Bell, Philadelphia, PA

White Water Falls in Oconee County, South Carolina

Inauguration of Governor Hodges

Visit to the Martin Luther King, Jr.'s birthplace and burial ground in Atlanta, Georgia

Martha Pough, aunt and Bessie Isaac, my mother

The eternal light memorial for Dr. Martin Luther King, Jr.

From 1619 – 2009

President Barack Hussein Obama is the 44th President of the United States. President Obama was elected the First African-American President of the United States on November 4, 2008, and sworn in on January 20, 2009.

President Obama was born in Hawaii on August 4, 1961. President Obama's father, Barack Obama Sr., was from Kenya; a country in Africa, and his mother, Ann Dunham, was from Kansas; a state in the United States.

President Obama was sworn in for his job in the presence of his wife, Michelle Obama, his two daughters, Malia and Sasha Obama, his mother-in-law, Marian Robinson, other family members, and witnessed by over a million viewers on the capitol grounds in Washington, D. C. This historical event was viewed all over the world. Read his history to find out more about the man who became the first African-American to become President of the United States.

President Obama's activated *Innate Genius Intelligent Abilities* led him to "work for the people" as the President of the United States of America.

Our son's Innate Genius Intelligent Abilities skills were taught to him in my womb. He has been taught to love, respect, provide for and marry your daughter. Raise your daughters to love, respect, and marry our sons. They need to work to take care of each other and take care of our grandchildren. Yes, we will help them.

About the Author

Mia Isaac was born in Columbia, South Carolina and reared in North, South Carolina and Brooklyn, New York. She was a teacher for 16 years; ten years in Brooklyn, New York, and six years in Columbia, South Carolina. Mia Isaac was educated at Long Island University in Brooklyn and Long Island University Graduate School, Fordham University, New York; Bishop College, Dallas, Texas; University of South Carolina and Columbia College, Columbia, South Carolina.

Mia Isaac's first publication, "I Cry For My Parents", was her first personal vision for loving, protecting, and educating the African-American child. She has appeared on television and radio programs within the state and travels to different states speaking to fathers, mothers and children about activating their innate genius intelligent abilities now and into the 21st Century.

She received an incentive award from Richland District #1 in the school year of 1988/89, received an award from parents in the school year of 1983/84 in Brooklyn, New York; organized and established the Youth and Parental Involvement Organization 1995 and teaches the IGIA Program 1991 and still currently teaches the program (2009).

GLOSSARY

The BIBLE: Read the Bible and apply the accurate knowledge daily.

PICTURES:

1. The photographers for pictures with the exception of pictures on pages 67, and 129 in the book were taken by Mia Isaac and Daniel Leon Isaac Jamison (son).

2. The photographers for pictures on page 129 are Melvin Tobin (cousin) and Brandon Shell (nephew).

Footnotes:

1. GRUSON, LINDSEY. "Colors Has Powerful Effect On Behavior, Researchers Assert." New York Times, October 19, 1982 p. C1, C7.
2. All names in the text pages 7-35 have been changed.

Dictionaries:

1. The Random House Dictionary
2. The American Heritage Dictionary
3. The Oxford English Dictionary
4. Funk and Wagnall's Standard Comprehensive International Dictionary
5. Webster's New World Dictionary
6. The New Columbia Encyclopedia

Put Parents First

IGIA
INNATE GENIUS INTELLIGENCE ABILITY
HAVE YOU READ THESE THREE BOOKS?

I CRY FOR MY PARENTS
Mia Isaac
49 pages, softbound- 1990
ISBN 978-0-9630229-0-3
Price $7.95
IGIA *Publishing & Distribution*
PO Box 3688
Columbia, SC 29203

ALPHABLACK CULTURE BEGINNING ACTIVITY BOOK
Mia Isaac
48 color pages, softbound – 1991
ISBN 978-0-9630229-1-1
Price $21.95
IGIA *Publishing & Distribution*
PO Box 3688
Columbia, SC 29203

**"MOMMIE WHAT IS A NIGGER?"
THE CASE OF THE CENTURIES**

Mia Isaac
280 pages, softbound – 1996
ISBN 978-0-9630229-2X
Price $20.95
IGIA *Publishing & Distribution*
PO Box 3688
Columbia, SC 29203

Mia Isaac: *Parent, Teacher, Researcher, Author, Photographer, & Consultant*
Email: *igiapublis@sc.rr.com*

www.ingramcontent.com/pod-product-compliance
Lightning Source LLC
Chambersburg PA
CBHW041550220426
43666CB00002B/22